HARNESSING ENERGY

NATURAL GAS POWER

BY DIANE BAILEY

CREATIVE PAPERBACKS

HARNESSING ENERGY • HARNESSING ENERGY •

TABLE OF CONTENTS

Introduction 4

CHAPTER 1 *God's Breath* 6

CHAPTER 2 *The Energy Highway* 14

CHAPTER 3 *Bridge to the Future* 22

CHAPTER 4 *Digging Deeper* 30

Moments in Natural Gas History 38

Glossary 42

Selected Bibliography 44

Websites 45

Read More 46

Index 47

INTRODUCTION

PEACE AND WAR. WEALTH AND POVERTY. PROGRESS AND SETBACKS. HISTORY HAS BROUGHT HUGE SWINGS IN THE HUMAN CONDITION, AND WITH EVERY CHOICE PEOPLE MAKE, THERE IS THE POTENTIAL TO MOVE FORWARD OR STEP BACKWARD. AT THE CORE OF THIS CONTINUAL STRUGGLE HAS BEEN THE QUEST FOR ENERGY. ENERGY GAVE HUMANS POWER AND MOTIVATED THEM TO DO GREAT THINGS—WITH BOTH POSITIVE AND NEGATIVE EFFECTS. WITHOUT ENERGY, PEOPLE WOULD NOT BE ABLE TO DRIVE CARS, OPERATE COMPUTERS, OR POWER FACTORIES. WARS ARE FOUGHT TRYING TO DOMINATE SOURCES OF ENERGY. FORTUNES ARE MADE AND LOST DEPENDING ON HOW THAT ENERGY IS MANAGED. THE LAWS OF PHYSICS STATE THAT ENERGY CANNOT BE CREATED OR DESTROYED. THAT IS TRUE, BUT ENERGY CAN BE HARNESSED AND DIRECTED. IT CAN BE WASTED, OR IT CAN BE COAXED INTO EFFICIENCY. CIVILIZATIONS AND TECHNOLOGIES HAVE LEAPED FORWARD—AND SOMETIMES BACKWARD—AS HUMANS HAVE TAPPED INTO EARTH'S SOURCES OF ENERGY.

Understanding the capabilities of natural gas has helped countries shift toward cleaner energy.

It took centuries for natural gas to be understood and even longer before it was appreciated. In the early days of oil exploration, there was no market for the natural gas that escaped as oil was extracted. In fact, **wildcatters** grumbled that the one thing worse than drilling a dry hole was finding gas instead. How could an invisible, floating substance be captured? It was even more daunting to think of how to use it. Gradually, however, observation prompted innovation. Gas burned—that much was obvious. Why not harness that energy? Once it had a purpose, natural gas became a lot more attractive. It would still require decades of technological tending to develop the market, but now it was worth the effort.

CHAPTER ONE

GOD'S BREATH

AN UNEARTHLY FORCE SEEMED TO BE AT WORK. Flames came shooting out of the ground, but their source was a mystery. Was it the work of God? Of the devil? Ancient peoples didn't know the answer. They thought that the very air itself was burning.

It wasn't, of course. There was something else mixed in the air—colorless, odorless natural gas that had escaped from underground.

The Chimera eternal flames in present-day Turkey are named for a mythological, fire-spouting beast.

Occasionally, lightning ignited these gas **seeps**, causing the ancient Greeks to believe a **divine** force was at work, creating what they called an "eternal flame." They even built temples on the spots where "God's Breath" seeped out of the ground. In China, 2,500 years ago, people figured out a way to use this gas. First, they channeled it through hollow bamboo poles. These poles led to a fire that boiled pots of seawater to extract the salt. Since then, the applications of natural gas have come a long way.

Today, natural gas is used to heat homes and businesses as well as to fuel electric power plants. It's an important **feedstock** for the chemical industry. Natural gas is used to make paper, metal, stone, clay, plastic, and glass. In North America, many food crops are grown with the help of an ammonia-based fertilizer. This fertilizer was produced with natural gas. Have leftovers from a restaurant? Get a take-home box made with ethylene, a chemical that comes from natural gas.

People have been using natural gas for thousands of years, but it has existed in the earth for much longer. Millions of years ago, decaying plants were buried in the earth. Layers of dirt and rocks pressed down on them, creating conditions of extreme heat and pressure. Over time, the compressed plant material turned into what are now called fossil fuels—coal, oil, and natural gas. Natural gas is usually found next to coal or oil, at depths of between 3,000 and 25,000 feet (914-7,620 m). Most of the world's known gas deposits were formed somewhere between 10 and 270 million years ago. The main ingredient in natural gas is methane, but it's often mixed with liquid **hydrocarbons** such as propane and butane. Natural gas in this state is called "wet gas." These liquid hydrocarbons must be separated from the methane before it can be used as "dry gas."

Sandstone is likened to a hard sponge because of its pores that trap oil, water, and natural gas.

Natural gas can be divided into the two broad categories of conventional and unconventional. Conventional gas is found in permeable rocks such as sandstone. Permeable rocks are not completely solid and can be penetrated by the gas. These rocks are sandwiched between layers of impermeable rocks, which cannot be penetrated. They keep the gas from escaping to the surface. Today, gas is being found in more unconventional places. Shale gas is found within a type of rock called shale. Shale is relatively impermeable, so the gas does not leak out. Tight gas is packed into sand or silt that is not **porous** enough to allow the gas to flow from one place to another. Unconventional deposits can hold large amounts of natural gas, but it's harder to extract it. Another type of unconventional gas is coalbed methane, which is found with coal deposits.

There are large deposits of natural gas in Russia and the United States. Together, these two countries are responsible for almost 40 percent of the natural gas produced worldwide. They are also the world's biggest consumers of natural gas. Turkmenistan, Iran, and Qatar also have very large reserves but do not produce as much of it. Estimates vary as to how much recoverable natural gas exists worldwide. The oil company British Petroleum (BP) reported more than 200 trillion cubic meters (261 trillion cubic yards) at the end of 2011. That would be enough to satisfy the world's population for more than 60 years. But the International Energy Agency (IEA) put the estimate much higher. It reported a number closer to 800 trillion cubic meters (1,046 trillion cubic yards). That amount could stretch for 250 years at our current rates of use. Unconventional gas sources account for the higher IEA figure, but such gas is harder to reach and more expensive. Scientists aren't sure how much of it can even be collected.

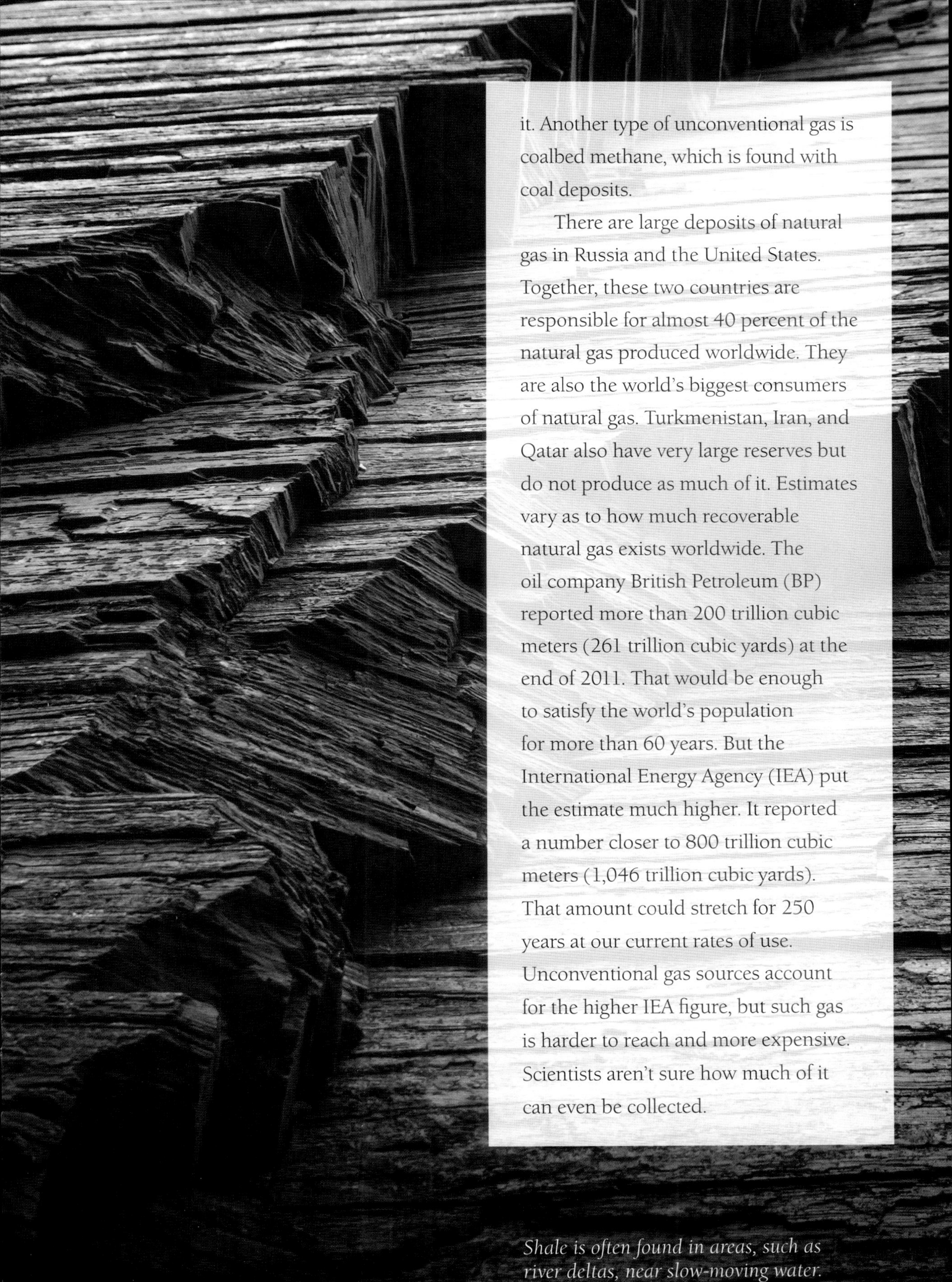

Shale is often found in areas, such as river deltas, near slow-moving water.

The history of natural gas really begins with its **predecessor**, coal gas. Coal gas can be produced by burning coal in a controlled atmosphere that is purposely low in oxygen. The exhaust is a man-made natural gas. Chemically, coal gas and natural gas are quite different. Natural gas produces more heat and burns more cleanly than coal gas. However, in the 19th and early 20th centuries, coal was the primary fuel source in countries such as the U.S. and Great Britain. It was easier to manufacture coal gas than it was to capture natural gas.

Still, people could not ignore the presence of natural gas, as it literally seeped out of the ground. In the 1600s, French explorers in America observed American Indians setting natural gas on fire. Near Niagara Falls in Canada, documents from 1794 report that burning springs could "boil a teakettle in 15 minutes." Children would toss burning embers at the seeps to watch the flames leap into the air. In the early 1800s, people in the U.S. decided to dig for it. The first natural gas wells were shallow, and early pipelines were crude and inefficient. In the 1860s, one writer concluded, "[Natural gas is] a worthless asset, inasmuch as the most fanciful person could not conceive of the piping of the gas a **sufficient** distance to make it a marketable **commodity**."

While there were some "early adopters" of natural gas, it was a long time before usage became widespread. At first, natural gas was considered a necessary evil when drilling for water or oil. It was not useful unless it could be transported, and there was no way to easily move gas around. Before the technology to capture and move natural gas evolved, people dealt with gas escaping from wells in another way. They lit it on fire and let it burn off naturally. These were called "flares."

By the late 19th century, drilling equipment improved, and pipelines got better, enabling natural gas to reach more places.

In the 1800s, Findlay, Ohio, was known as the "City of Light" because of the gas flares from its Karg Well.

People also learned more about **geology**, which helped them locate new deposits of oil and gas. In 1891, the first pipeline to go beyond the boundaries of a single city was built. It extended about 120 miles (193 km), from gas fields in Indiana to customers in Chicago, Illinois. Previous coal gas pipelines had been built for local use alone. Now the first lines were in place for a national network. Still, it wasn't until the late 1940s, after World War II, that things really got moving. Early pipelines were made of wood or iron. Improvements in welding techniques and **metallurgy** allowed for the construction of longer, stronger pipelines made of steel. Pipelines were built in Europe in the 1960s, allowing gas to be transported through towns and into individual homes. Today, the world's pipeline network is a gigantic steel spiderweb, not limited to single countries or continents. It connects gas fields in Russia to customers in Europe. Gas from the Gulf of Mexico is pumped hundreds of miles north to New England.

With the problem of transportation solved, natural gas producers were able to sell their product more easily. In homes, it was used to heat water and provide electricity. It was also used to make various products in industry. Previously, coal had been the primary fuel for electric power plants. But natural gas worked, too. "King Coal" now had a competitor.

Gas travels through under- or aboveground pipelines and even over rivers in pipeline bridges.

5,8 m
5,5 m

CHAPTER TWO

THE ENERGY HIGHWAY

IT BURNS IN THE LITTLE BLUE FLAME ON THE STOVE. It's the giant flare that can be seen from a space shuttle orbiting miles above Earth. It fuels the tiny fire that heats a teakettle or burns in massive quantities to power a gas **turbine** at an electric power plant. It can be compressed into tanks to be used as fuel for cars, or it can be chemically split to produce hydrogen for industrial uses.

Natural gas is versatile and reliable. Those qualities have made it a steady contributor to the world's fuel supply for decades. Today, its popularity is increasing. New discoveries of gas supplies

Natural gas-fueled kitchen stoves heat up quickly and use less energy than their electric counterparts.

Incidents of gas flaring in states such as North Dakota increased in 2013.

have lowered the price, and concerns over pollution from coal make natural gas seem more attractive. As countries pass new laws that limit pollution, natural gas becomes an even bigger part of the energy economy. Natural gas-fired electric plants began to come online in the 1970s. By 2000, almost every new electric power plant in the U.S. was run on natural gas. Today, about 20 percent of the world's electricity is generated by natural gas, and gas makes up the same percentage of the overall energy supply.

Natural gas is often touted as the "clean" fossil fuel. It's not as energy-dense as coal or oil, but it is much cleaner to burn. Fewer chemicals are released in the exhaust, or the fumes created when something is burned. It also produces less carbon dioxide, which is the main **greenhouse gas** contributing to **global warming**. However, environmentalists point out that gas has its drawbacks. It may be cleaner-burning, but what about before that? Chemicals are used during the drilling process that can contaminate surrounding soil and water. Land is torn up to produce a drilling site. If a well leaks, methane is released straight into the air. There's not as much methane as there is carbon dioxide, but as greenhouse gases go, it's 20 times worse. Opponents to natural gas argue that these side effects must be considered when determining how "clean" gas is.

Seismic readings show Earth's vibrations, helping engineers learn the depth and location of underground formations.

Coal stays in one place. Oil may move, but at least it's visible. Gas, on the other hand, is sneaky. Capturing it has posed technical challenges ever since people first discovered it. To extract it successfully, engineers need to know their physics and have armloads of geological data at their disposal. If they drill in the wrong place, they may let the gas escape into the air, wasting the resource and polluting the air, or they might never reach it at all and leave empty-handed.

The first step is finding the gas. To do that, scientists need to know what kind of rocks they're dealing with. One clue in identifying rocks is their density. Engineers use magnetic readings, gravity measurements, and **seismic** imaging to help determine density. Then they can determine the type of rocks, and whether they are likely to contain natural gas.

At a traditional gas well, workers drill into the ground until they hit a reserve of natural gas. This is sometimes called a "kitchen" and is more pressurized than the surface of the earth. According to the laws of physics, when an area with lower pressure connects with one of higher pressure, the material in the higher-pressure space will flow into the lower-pressure one. That evens things out. Thus, the gas flows into the well as it equalizes pressure.

Drilling for gas (or oil) can be damaging to the land around it. It typically requires several acres of land to set up a drill pad, which is the area that includes the rig and other equipment used for drilling. Rocks, debris, and mud from the drilling process can litter the area. However, drilling methods and equipment are steadily improving. Thinner bores (like drill bits) can now do the jobs that previously required thicker ones. In the past, workers sometimes had to drill in several spots to get all the gas out of a field. Now they use flexible tubes that can "turn" underground, so they do not have to drill a new hole at the surface. Underground, horizontal drilling reduces the "drilling footprint"—the amount of land required on the surface—lessening damage to the land.

Once the gas is collected, it's compressed so that more will fit into a smaller space. Then it's injected into the pipeline. At these higher pressures, the heavier liquid hydrocarbons **condense** out of the gas, but the gas loses pressure as it travels. Compressor stations located along the pipeline remove the liquids and return the gas to a high pressure, and the journey continues.

Polycrystalline diamond compact (PDC) drill bits are commonly used for drilling into shale.

Often, gas is found next to oil, but sometimes it's too difficult to build a pipeline to transport the gas from there. In the past, this gas would have been flared (burned off). Now, though, it can be converted into a liquid by cooling it to -260 °F (-162 °C). Liquefied natural gas (LNG) takes up much less space–only about 1/600th the volume. Special tankers can transport LNG in and out of areas where there are no pipelines, but high-tech containers are needed to keep it cool. (If it warms up too quickly, it can explode.) The ports through which tankers of LNG move must be specially outfitted to deal with the material. Once LNG reaches land, it's reconverted into a gas and handed over to the pipeline. LNG is expensive to move, but in some cases it makes economic sense.

Specialized tank ships for transporting liquefied natural gas can be up to 1,000 feet (304.8 m) long.

Japan is a big consumer of LNG. Japan has no fossil fuels of its own. Because it's an island, the natural gas pipeline system can't reach it. Japan imports its LNG from Indonesia and the Middle East. LNG is also widely used in Taiwan and South Korea, and to some extent in the U.S. and Europe.

Today, the focus of natural gas is often on unconventional sources, such as shale gas and tight gas, and finding ways to safely and economically extract it. Extracting shale gas uses a technology called hydraulic fracturing, better known as "fracking." In this process, water, chemicals, and another material (often sand) are injected into rocks containing natural gas. This makes the rock crack. Then the water is sucked back up. The sand stays behind to prop open the cracks and let the gas flow out.

Experiments with hydraulic fracturing first started in the 1940s, but it wasn't until the late 1990s that it became widely used. Energy companies soon explored combinations involving both fracking and horizontal drilling. Such methods let them recover large amounts of shale gas that had been trapped underground.

In the early 2000s, this process allowed drilling companies to recover huge amounts of gas from a deposit in Texas called the Barnett Shale. After that success, developers turned their eye to the staggering quantities of gas believed to reside in the Marcellus Shale beneath the northeastern states. In 2012, president Barack Obama announced, "We have a supply of natural gas that can last America nearly 100 years."

Not everyone shares a rosy view when it comes to shale gas. David Hughes, a Canadian geoscientist, warned in 2013 that shale deposits are uneven in quality and could be tapped out quickly. He wrote, "Although some wells can be extremely productive, they are typically a small percentage of the total and are concentrated in sweet spots." In addition, fracking is a very controversial technique. Some evidence suggests it can leave behind toxic chemicals in water. There is also the possibility of leaking natural gas into the air. Nonetheless, shale gas is a potentially vast resource, and nations such as Russia, China, and Australia are increasing their production. How countries decide to use it—or not—will likely shape the future of the natural gas industry.

Operating fracking and other drilling sites is a highly dangerous but often high-paying job (opposite).

CHAPTER THREE

BRIDGE TO THE FUTURE

NATURAL GAS IS SOMETIMES CALLED THE "BRIDGE" BETWEEN FOSSIL FUELS AND **RENEWABLE** FORMS OF ENERGY. Like its siblings oil and coal, natural gas is something the earth isn't making any more of—not quickly, anyway. People won't be able to use it forever. However, we currently don't have the technology or **infrastructure** to switch completely to renewable power sources, such as solar or wind energy. Even if it were fast-tracked, that conversion would require a lot of money. It would also take a lot of time—not just years but decades.

The complex U.S. natural gas network contains more than 305,000 miles (490,850 km) of pipeline.

Natural gas, on the other hand, is cheap, available, and plentiful (at least for now). It can compete with oil to fuel cars and with coal to produce electricity. Recent and future environmental regulations to reduce pollution call for coal plants to install new equipment. Coal will probably become more expensive as a result, making gas even more attractive. It's cleaner than coal, cheaper than nuclear, and it can produce a lot of power *now*. Nations all over the world are counting on natural gas to be a heavy lifter in their future energy requirements. And, as technology improves, it's likely to find even more applications. For example, in 2011, scientists at the American technology company Honeywell announced a new way to convert methane directly into ethylene. Ethylene is a main ingredient in plastics. This could make the plastics industry an even bigger customer for natural gas. Natural gas does have drawbacks, but it's terribly useful stuff. In fact, many environmentalists worry that natural gas is so appealing that it could *delay* the transition away from fossil fuels.

Electric power generation represents a huge market for natural gas. It's not that gas is the only fuel capable of running a power plant. Coal, hydroelectric, and nuclear power are all capable of doing the job. But they all have problems: Coal is dirty. Hydro is limited to places where a large dam can be built (and most of those locations are already used up). Nuclear is expensive and comes with serious safety concerns.

Meanwhile, the world's demand for electricity is growing. It's especially significant in developing countries such as China. That nation

Interest in alternative fuels has increased as both the cost of oil and public awareness of energy issues have risen.

Hybrids similar to the German CNG-powered Opel Corsa can run on both natural gas and regular gasoline.

could more than double the amount of natural gas it requires by 2017. Demand probably won't be quite as strong in Europe, because several countries have invested more in renewable energy. Coal is currently the world's most common fuel for electricity generation, but gas is gaining ground. The IEA predicts that, by 2017, gas use could increase over its current levels by about 15 percent worldwide, and it will be especially important in generating electricity.

Most transportation fuel, such as diesel and gasoline, is made from oil. Cars and trucks work best with liquid fuels, which are easily refined from crude oil. But natural gas is making inroads in transportation fuel. One option is to turn it into a liquid. However, to remain stable, LNG must be kept at an extremely low temperature. This requires complicated storage tanks and cooling systems to be built onto cars. Another option would be to compress the gas so that more can be carried. In the end, that may make more sense if natural gas is to be used in vehicles on an everyday basis.

As part of its goal to phase out fossil fuels by 2050, Iceland began using hydrogen fuel cell buses in 2003.

Natural gas cars are used today, but they are not widespread over the globe. One drawback is that natural gas is not as energy-dense as gasoline, so these cars can't travel as far. Also, there aren't many natural gas fuel stations located along the freeway. But that doesn't mean they won't appear in the future. Karl Rose, the director of Policy and Scenarios at the World Energy Council, said in 2012, "There's no reason [natural gas transport] couldn't catch on in the emerging world. Asians are starting off fresh without the dedication to diesel that exists in the European transport sector." Another plus is that it's relatively easy to convert a traditional gasoline-burning car into a natural gas-burning car.

Natural gas could also be used as feedstock for cars or other machines that are powered by hydrogen. Since the 1990s, there has been increased talk about a hydrogen-based economy. In this scenario, hydrogen would be used to carry energy through systems called fuel cells. Hydrogen burns much more cleanly than traditional fossil fuels. However,

Clumps of methane hydrates look like snow and melt at room temperature, releasing flammable methane.

hydrogen would not be the source of the energy. Instead, it would be manufactured by using another feedstock, possibly coal or natural gas. Thus, fossil fuels could still be burned in order to make another kind of energy. Such a process is not only expensive, but right now it uses more energy than it produces. However, if the technology could be improved, it would be a cleaner option.

Another place to find methane—natural gas's main ingredient—is in methane hydrates. These are methane **molecules** combined with water molecules. Methane hydrates look like ice, and they exist at cold temperatures. Studies show that the earth has tremendous stores of methane hydrates in the Arctic as well as under the ocean. When the hydrates warm up, they come apart

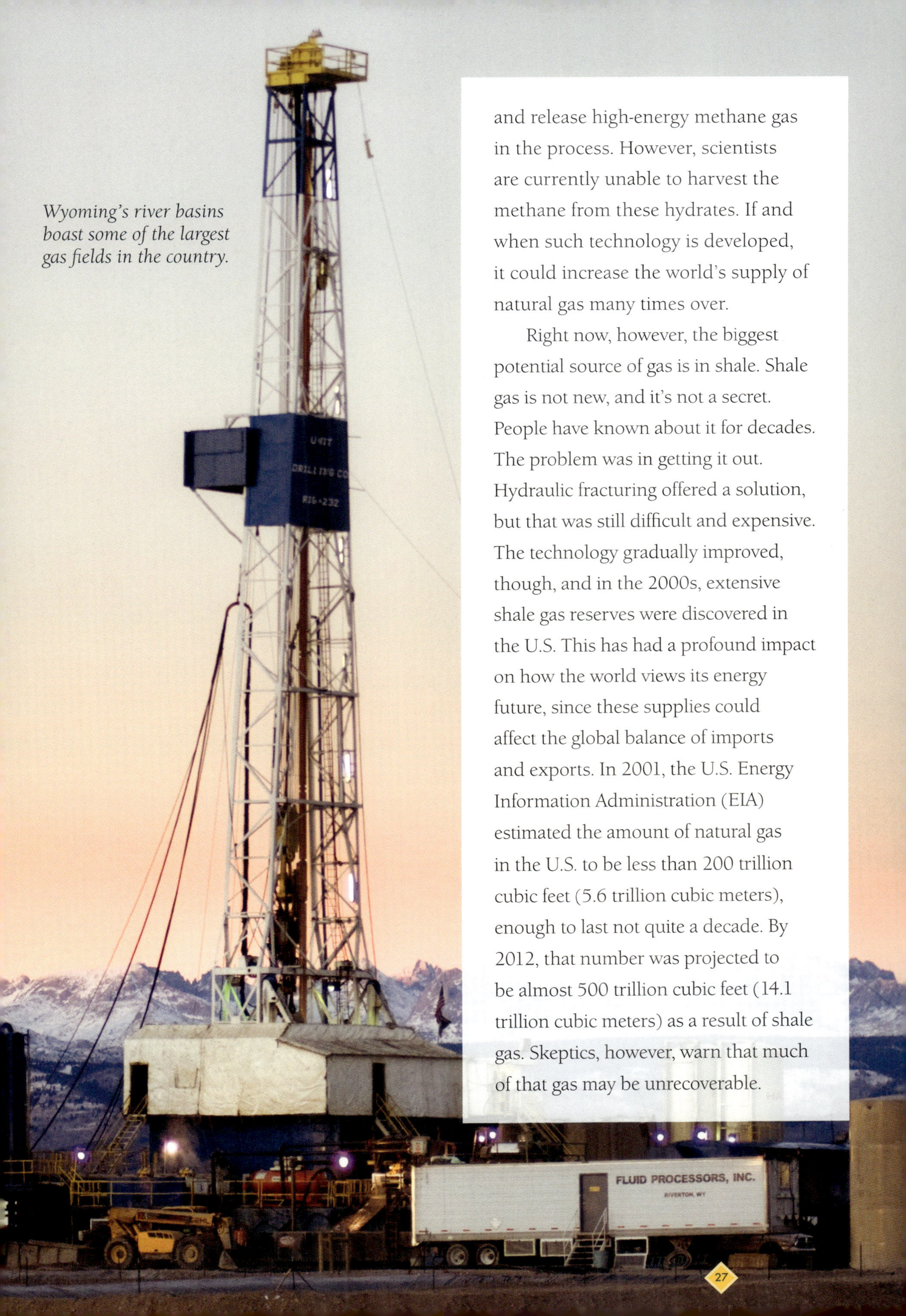

Wyoming's river basins boast some of the largest gas fields in the country.

and release high-energy methane gas in the process. However, scientists are currently unable to harvest the methane from these hydrates. If and when such technology is developed, it could increase the world's supply of natural gas many times over.

Right now, however, the biggest potential source of gas is in shale. Shale gas is not new, and it's not a secret. People have known about it for decades. The problem was in getting it out. Hydraulic fracturing offered a solution, but that was still difficult and expensive. The technology gradually improved, though, and in the 2000s, extensive shale gas reserves were discovered in the U.S. This has had a profound impact on how the world views its energy future, since these supplies could affect the global balance of imports and exports. In 2001, the U.S. Energy Information Administration (EIA) estimated the amount of natural gas in the U.S. to be less than 200 trillion cubic feet (5.6 trillion cubic meters), enough to last not quite a decade. By 2012, that number was projected to be almost 500 trillion cubic feet (14.1 trillion cubic meters) as a result of shale gas. Skeptics, however, warn that much of that gas may be unrecoverable.

Increased deposits of natural gas could also help the LNG market. At one point, it looked as though the U.S. would have to import LNG to meet its needs. Now facilities built for imports are being retrofitted to handle exports. Other countries are also stepping up production of LNG. Australia has large stores of coalbed methane, which it is converting to LNG and exporting to Asia. Russia's LNG market is also expected to grow.

A 2011 report from the IEA predicted that the next few decades would be "a golden age for gas." By 2035, the report concluded, natural gas would supply 25 percent of the world's total energy needs. That represents a 4 percent increase from the total usage in 2011. The exploding population and economy

When demand for natural gas is high, prices rise, and gas is used rather than injected into storage tanks.

in China would be one reason. So would a decrease in nuclear power or an increase in natural gas-powered vehicles. The report also predicted that demand would increase four-fold in India and nearly double in the Middle East. Of that demand, more than 40 percent is expected to come from unconventional gas sources, such as shale gas.

Scientists have found new supplies of natural gas and new ways to use it. What they haven't yet found is a way to change its basic definition. Natural gas is still a fossil fuel, and it still has the problems associated with that. Faith Birol, one of the authors of the IEA study, noted, "We are not saying that it will be a golden age for humanity—we are saying it will be a golden age for gas."

CHAPTER FOUR

DIGGING DEEPER

THE SUPPLIES ARE THERE. There's an infrastructure in place. Natural gas is cheap and reliable. What's not to like? Producers of natural gas would probably say nothing! But others are more skeptical. Environmentalists point out that natural gas is still a fossil fuel that pollutes. And it will eventually run out—the only

question is when. Using it as a crutch now could just make things worse down the road, when it can't be a fallback fuel. Some worry it's being presented as a long-term energy solution. Marty Spitzer, the U.S. climate policy director for the World Wildlife Fund, asked in 2012, "Just because we have the gas, just because we know how to use it, does that really mean we should?" He advocates using gas along with other forms of renewable energies.

If the IEA is correct, natural gas usage is going to surge over the next 20 years. That will have various effects on the environment. It's true that natural gas doesn't emit as much carbon dioxide as other fossil fuels. If gas is used extensively in electrical power plants and automobiles, then overall carbon dioxide emissions could fall. On the other hand, more natural gas could decrease usage of nuclear power—and that would lead to higher emissions.

Installing gas-powered generation units in Russian thermal power plants helps reduce carbon dioxide emissions.

Emissions come at the end of the cycle, when natural gas is being burned. But there are other negative environmental effects that happen earlier in the process. Earth took millions of years to make coal, oil, and natural gas, and it does not give them up easily. Drilling for gas is an aggressive process that's hard on the land. Acres of land are used up for drill pads, wells, and roads. Tons of rock and debris are strewn about as drill bits bore down to reach the gas deposits. More ground is torn up for the construction of pipelines.

Pipeline construction and drilling equipment can cause forest fragmentation, displacing native wildlife species.

Drilling is dirty, noisy, and invasive, and that's just for a traditional well. Accessing shale gas is even harder, and environmental side effects may be even more dire. Shale gas drilling requires a network of wells, spread over large areas of land. The long-term effect of tampering with the geological makeup of the earth is not known. Some scientists believe that fracking could cause instability in the earth's crust and lead to earthquakes.

Fracking also uses millions of gallons of fresh water. That's enough to affect the water supplies people depend on for drinking and other household uses. Also, the water used in fracking is mixed with a variety of chemicals. Many of them are toxic. They can stay in the water unless it's specially treated.

Fracking is blamed for the methane in a Pennsylvania well that made water flammable and residents ill.

Unfortunately, such treatments are often technically complex and beyond the reach of normal wastewater processing plants.

Some of those chemicals may also seep into the groundwater. In the 2000s, companies began fracking in the Marcellus Shale. The process soon came under intense observation. Residents in New York and Pennsylvania discovered that they could literally light their tap water on fire. It turned out that there was methane in the water. Scientists do not know for sure if the methane leaked in during fracking, but it is possible. The mere possibility is enough to cause many people to demand that fracking be halted, at least until the consequences can be better understood. Engineer Mario Salazar served as a technical expert with the U.S. Environmental Protection Agency. "In 10 to 100 years we are going to find out that most of our groundwater is polluted," he predicted.

The flammability of natural gas poses other dangers. Transporting and storing gas must happen under special conditions. If a tanker of LNG exploded, it could kill everything nearby and damage buildings up to a mile away, according to a 2004 study by U.S. government scientists. That could make these tankers vulnerable to terrorists who could blow them up. Pipelines are also easy targets.

In January 2007, thousands of nearby residents were evacuated as Chinese firefighters controlled leakage from an LNG truck.

Hundreds of thousands of miles of pipelines run underground. It's impossible to monitor every inch of them. **Saboteurs** could disrupt gas supplies or use it as a potential weapon.

Much of the world's natural gas resources are located in or travel through areas that are politically unstable. For example, a lot of natural gas is produced in the Middle Eastern countries of Qatar and Yemen. It's then carried to Europe on tankers that must pass through the Suez Canal, which borders politically unstable Egypt. Problems in Libya and Nigeria resulted in supplies of LNG being held up in the 2010s. In 2009, during a price dispute, Russia simply cut off gas exports to Ukraine. This affected several European nations that depended on gas coming through Ukraine, and it led European Union leaders to question whether they should continue to rely on Russia for one-third of their gas in the coming decades.

All of this ties into the idea of energy security. Many countries want to be self-sufficient when it comes to energy. They do not want to depend on imports from other nations. Using a **domestic** source of energy means they won't have to negotiate with other countries to buy fuel. There is less chance of the price going up without warning or of the supply being cut off entirely. When political relations become tense, having a domestic source of energy offers a form of independence. It also makes it cheaper, because transportation costs are lower.

Gas is increasingly "going global." The world's largest supplies of natural gas are found in Russia and the Middle East. France also appears to have huge reserves. But the deposits are not always located near where the gas is needed. Natural gas is increasingly used to fuel electrical power plants. Most electrical use is in the U.S. and Western Europe, although developing countries such as China and India are catching up fast. To funnel gas to these consumers, people need better ways of transporting the gas, either through pipelines or in liquid form.

How that infrastructure develops will depend on many factors. Cost, of course, is one. It's a huge project to build a broad and efficient network of pipelines, factories, tankers, ports, and storage facilities. Such a feat could cost several trillion dollars. Some experts expect to see a shift in the role of governments. Traditionally, governments have provided regulatory oversight as well as money to help build pipelines and other infrastructure. But as the industry grows, the financial burden may shift to private investors and companies. The amount of money invested in gas might grow, or it might

China's cross-country natural gas project involves several massive pipelines.

Construction of the Iran-Pakistan Pipeline, called the "Peace Pipeline," was estimated to cost $7.5 billion.

shrink. It will all depend on market factors, including the price of gas and the expected demand. However, it's likely that countries that encourage private investment will do better. In Qatar, for example, the industry has grown because the political and business climate stabilized.

Until renewables can provide significant amounts of power, natural gas will continue to play with the "big boys"—coal and nuclear. Coal isn't likely to die any time soon, although it will eventually run out. In the 1990s, nuclear was presented as a better option than coal or natural gas. But that view has changed in the last two decades. First, natural gas got cheaper. And the most recent incident to jeopardize nuclear's future was a disastrous accident at a nuclear power plant in Japan in 2011.

Over the last century, gas has grown up. Once, it was a nuisance. Untold amounts of energy were simply burned up during the quest to reach oil. Now it has become a valuable resource on its own. People know the problems with fossil fuels, but they will depend on them until renewables can take up the slack. The "eternal flame" of natural gas isn't truly eternal. But as the world transitions from fossil fuels, it may prove to be a lifeline.

In 1821, a gunsmith named William Hart went looking for gas. He had seen bubbles erupting from a stream near his home in Fredonia, New York. Hart drilled three times in a failed water well before he hit gas. His well was only 27 feet (8.2 m) deep! Often remembered as "the father of natural gas," Hart was piping the gas to local businesses by 1825. European geologist Baron Alexander von Humboldt called the effort "the eighth wonder of the world." In 1858, the Fredonia Gas Light & Water Company was formed, becoming the country's first natural gas corporation.

George Westinghouse kept the patent office busy. The American inventor is primarily known for his work in electricity, but he also applied his expertise to natural gas. After finding gas on the grounds of his Pittsburgh home, Westinghouse went into the gas business. In 1884 and 1885, he filed for dozens of patents related to the collection, transportation, and distribution of natural gas. He had ideas for how to improve drilling methods, prevent gas leaks, and measure gas flow through meters. Perhaps his most important development was a system that regulated the pressure of gas in pipelines. He later used this method for transporting electricity.

Westinghouse's work with natural gas made him realize the importance of transformers in electricity distribution and led to his invention of a high-voltage AC generator (above).

To keep supplies of natural gas steady, companies must keep large amounts of it in storage, ready to go when demand increases. Sometimes it's stored in tanks or in the pipeline system. But the better solution is to put it underground, where there's a lot more room. In 1915, natural gas was first successfully stored underground in Ontario, Canada. The gas was pumped into old gas fields that had been drilled and were now empty. Depleted gas fields have the geological characteristics necessary to hold the gas in the first place, so they are ideal places for storage. Underground **aquifers** and salt caverns are also used.

In 1937, the New London, Texas, school board decided to cancel its contract to buy natural gas. Instead, it voted to connect the school to a pipeline that vented exhaust gas from an oil well. What no one knew was that the line was leaking. A deadly store of natural gas was building up underneath the school. The gas exploded one day. It killed 300 people and destroyed the school. After the tragedy, the state of Texas required a chemical called mercaptan to be added to the gas. Mercaptan has a distinctive, unpleasant odor, like rotten eggs. If another leak occurred, people would smell it before disaster struck.

An underground natural gas storage facility contains surface equipment (above) that is used for both injecting gas into the reservoir and withdrawing gas when demand is high.

MOMENTS IN

The *Methane Pioneer* set sail in 1959, traveling from Louisiana to Great Britain. The world's first LNG tanker was loaded with more than 177,000 cubic feet (5,000 cubic meters) of liquefied natural gas. The successful voyage proved LNG could be safely transported. It jump-started the global trade in LNG, and two more tankers were built—the *Methane Princess* and the *Methane Progress*. In 1964, Algeria opened a commercial factory for liquefying natural gas and began exporting it to Great Britain. A decade after the *Methane Pioneer* first set out, it also became the first ship to bring imported LNG to the U.S.

Hydraulic fracturing was first used in the 1940s, but its value for harvesting shale gas was realized much later. In 1997, Mitchell Energy tried "slickwater" fracturing in the Barnett Shale, a large gas deposit in Texas. Other fracking methods used gels and large amounts of sand. The thick solution made it more difficult to pump the water at high speeds and for long distances. Slickwater is more slippery because it has chemicals added to it to reduce friction. It traveled through the shale rock more easily to fracture it and loosen the gas. This type of fracking was less expensive and made extracting the shale gas economical.

With the rapid growth of natural gas usage, LNG shipping has become an important market (left). Countries and oil companies have teamed to reduce gas flaring (center).

A flare from a gas well, burning into the night, can be seen miles above the earth's surface. It's an impressive sight. It's also a reminder that a large amount of natural gas is burned for no other reason than to get rid of it. In 2002, the World Bank started the Global Gas Flaring Reduction Initiative. The goal was to reduce the waste of natural gas. Satellite data collected between 1994 and 2009 showed that Russia and Nigeria flared off the most natural gas. Since records started being kept, both countries have cut back. The initiative has also placed an emphasis on educating people in developing countries about gas flares.

France may have huge stores of shale gas in the ground, but the government was concerned about using hydraulic fracturing to extract it. In 2011, France became the first nation to outlaw fracking. As of 2013, this controversial technique was the only way to effectively extract shale gas. Oil and gas companies objected to the regulation, arguing that France should tap into its gas supplies. But the government said the practice was unproven and potentially too dangerous, because the chemicals used could pollute drinking water. Until an alternative to fracking was developed, the French government was resolved the gas would stay in the ground.

Members of the Greens political group protested fracking during the 2012 European Parliament session (right), claiming the environmental damage wasn't worth potential benefits.

GLOSSARY

aquifers—underground deposits of water contained in permeable rock or other material

commodity—an item that is produced and sold

condense—to change from a gas into a liquid

divine—related to God or a deity

domestic—within any given nation; not involving other countries

emission—a gas given off as part of a chemical process

feedstock—a raw material or ingredient

geology—the study of rocks and the physical formation of the earth

global warming—the phenomenon of Earth's average temperatures increasing over time

greenhouse gas—a gas that builds up in Earth's atmosphere and prevents the release of heat

hydrocarbons—substances containing only hydrogen and carbon but in different proportions

infrastructure—the services and mechanisms used to support a society

metallurgy—the practice of working with and producing products from metals

molecule—two or more atoms that are chemically combined

porous—containing small spaces; spongelike or absorbent

predecessor—something that came before in a timeline or sequence; a forerunner

renewable—able to be replenished and used indefinitely

saboteur—someone who deliberately undermines or destroys a thing or process

seeps—places in the earth's crust where natural gas escapes

seismic—related to geological movement

sufficient—enough, adequate

turbine—a machine that is driven by water, steam, or a gas flowing through the blades of a wheel

wildcatter—a person who drills for oil or gas in areas not known to have resources

SELECTED BIBLIOGRAPHY

Gilardoni, Andrea. *The World Market for Natural Gas: Implications for Europe*. Berlin: Springer-Verlag, 2008.

Inkpen, Andrew, and Michael H. Moffett. *The Global Oil and Gas Industry: Management, Strategy, and Finance*. Tulsa, Okla.: PennWell Corporation, 2011.

Lustgarten, Abraham, and ProPublica. "Are Fracking Wastewater Wells Poisoning the Ground Beneath Our Feet?" *Scientific American*, June 21, 2012.

Motavalli, Jim. "Natural Gas Signals a Manufacturing Renaissance." *New York Times*, April 10, 2012.

Speight, J. G. *Natural Gas: A Basic Handbook*. Houston, Tex.: Gulf Publishing, 2007.

Waples, David A. *The Natural Gas Industry in Appalachia: A History from the First Discovery to the Maturity of the Industry*. Jefferson, N.C.: McFarland & Company, 2005.

"World Energy Outlook 2011: Are We Entering a Golden Age of Gas?" International Energy Agency, 2011.

Zeller, Tom. "Studies Say Natural Gas Has Its Own Environmental Problems." *New York Times*, April 11, 2011.

W E B S I T E S

Energy Quest: The Energy Story

http://energyquest.ca.gov/story/index.html

Several forms of energy are explored on this site, tracking the history of their usage and the technologies employed in harvesting or creating them.

U.S. Energy Information Administration

http://www.eia.gov/kids/energy.cfm?page=natural_gas_home-basics

This section of the U.S. Energy Information Administration's website provides information on how natural gas is found, how the resource is used, and its environmental impacts.

NOTE: *Every effort has been made to ensure that the websites listed above are suitable for children, that they have educational value, and that they contain no inappropriate material. However, because of the nature of the Internet, it is impossible to guarantee that these sites will remain active indefinitely or that their contents will not be altered.*

READ MORE

Gunderson, Jessica. *The Energy Dilemma*. Mankato, Minn.: Creative Education, 2011.

Morris, Neil. *The Energy Mix*. Mankato, Minn.: Smart Apple Media, 2010.

———. *Fossil Fuels*. Mankato, Minn.: Smart Apple Media, 2010.

Rooney, Anne. *Reducing the Carbon Footprint*. Mankato, Minn.: Smart Apple Media, 2010.

Royston, Angela. *Sustainable Energy*. Mankato, Minn.: Arcturus, 2009.

Solway, Andrew. *Climate Change*. Mankato, Minn.: Smart Apple Media, 2010.

Walker, Denise. *Fuel and the Environment*. Mankato, Minn.: Smart Apple Media, 2008.

INDEX

A
Asia 7, 9, 12, 19, 21, 23, 28, 29, 35, 36, 41
  China 7, 21, 23, 29, 36
  India 29, 36
  Japan 19, 37
  Russia 9, 12, 21, 28, 35, 36, 41
Australia 21, 28

B
British Petroleum (BP) 9

C
Canada 11, 39
components 8, 15, 17, 23, 26, 28, 34
  hydrocarbons 8, 17
  methane 8, 15, 23, 26, 28, 34

D
deposits 8, 9, 12, 21, 28, 32, 34, 36, 40
  Barnett Shale 21, 40
  Marcellus Shale 21, 34
drawbacks 15, 16, 17, 21, 23, 30–35, 39, 41
  environmental effects 15, 16, 17, 21, 30–34, 41
  flammability 34, 39
  political disputes 35
  weapon potential 35

E
early applications 5, 7, 11–12, 38
Energy Information Administration (EIA) 27
Environmental Protection Agency (EPA) 34
Europe 11, 12, 19, 24, 35, 36, 40, 41
  France 36, 41
  Great Britain 11, 40

F
fossil fuels 8, 9, 11, 12, 15, 16, 17, 18, 22, 23, 24, 25, 28, 29, 30–31, 32, 37, 39, 41

H
Hart, William 38
Honeywell 23

I
International Energy Agency (IEA) 9, 24, 28–29, 31

M
Middle East 9, 19, 29, 35, 36, 37

N
natural gas collection 5, 15–17, 19, 21, 32–34, 38, 40, 41
  compression 17
  drilling 5, 15, 16, 17, 21, 32–33, 38
  fracking 19, 21, 33–34, 40, 41
natural gas formation 8
natural gas storage 24, 34, 36, 39
natural gas types 8–9, 19, 21, 27, 28, 29, 33, 40, 41
  coalbed methane 9, 28
  shale 8, 19, 21, 27, 29, 33, 40, 41
  tight 8, 19
natural gas usage 7, 9, 12, 14, 15, 23–25, 29, 36
  in electric power plants 7, 12, 14, 15, 23, 36
Nigeria 35, 41
nuclear power 23, 29, 31, 37

O
Obama, Barack 21

P
physical features 5, 6

R
regulations 15, 23, 36, 41
  Global Gas Flaring Reduction Initiative 41
renewable energy 22, 24, 31, 37

T
transportation of natural gas 11, 12, 17–19, 24, 25, 28, 34–36, 38, 40
  liquefied natural gas (LNG) 18–19, 24, 28, 34, 35, 40
  pipelines 12, 17–18, 19, 32, 34–35, 36, 38

U
United States 9, 11, 15, 19, 21, 27, 28, 36, 39, 40

W
Westinghouse, George 38
World Energy Council 25
World Wildlife Fund 31

HARNESSING ENERGY • HARNESSING ENERGY •

Published by Creative Paperbacks
P.O. Box 227, Mankato, Minnesota 56002
Creative Paperbacks is an imprint of The Creative Company
www.thecreativecompany.us

Design and production by The Design Lab
Art direction by Rita Marshall
Printed in the United States of America

Photographs by Alamy (Chronicle, epa european pressphoto agency b.v., Everett Collection Inc, Mar Photographics, Gabe Palmer, Radharc Images, Robert Harding Picture Library Ltd), Corbis (Car Culture, Ashley Cooper, Imaginechina, Vahid Salemi/AP, Les Stone, Mark Thiessen/National Geographic Society, Ted Wood/Aurora Photos, Zhang Yong/Xinhua Press), Dreamstime (Oleksandr Kalinichenko), Shutterstock (alexan55, bikeriderlondon, Sissy Borbely, Cardaf, cherezoff, Cico, Glovatskiy, Leonid Ikan, Jackiso, Oleksandr Kalinichenko, Kekyalyaynen, Kesu, leungchopan, Oleg - F, Zeljko Radojko, Matt Ragen, sigur, ssuaphotos)

Library of Congress Cataloging-in-Publication Data
Bailey, Diane.
Natural gas power / Diane Bailey.
p. cm. — (Harnessing energy)
Includes bibliographical references and index.
Summary: An examination of the ways in which natural gas has historically been used as an energy source and how current and future energy demands are changing its technical applications and efficiency levels.
ISBN 978-1-60818-409-5 (hardcover)
ISBN 978-0-89812-995-3 (pbk)
1. Gas as fuel—Juvenile literature. 2. Gas power plants—Juvenile literature. 3. Natural gas—Juvenile literature. I. Title.

TP350.B155 2014
553.2'85—dc23 2013035754

CCSS: RI.5.1, 2, 3, 4, 8, 9

First Edition
9 8 7 6 5 4 3 2 1